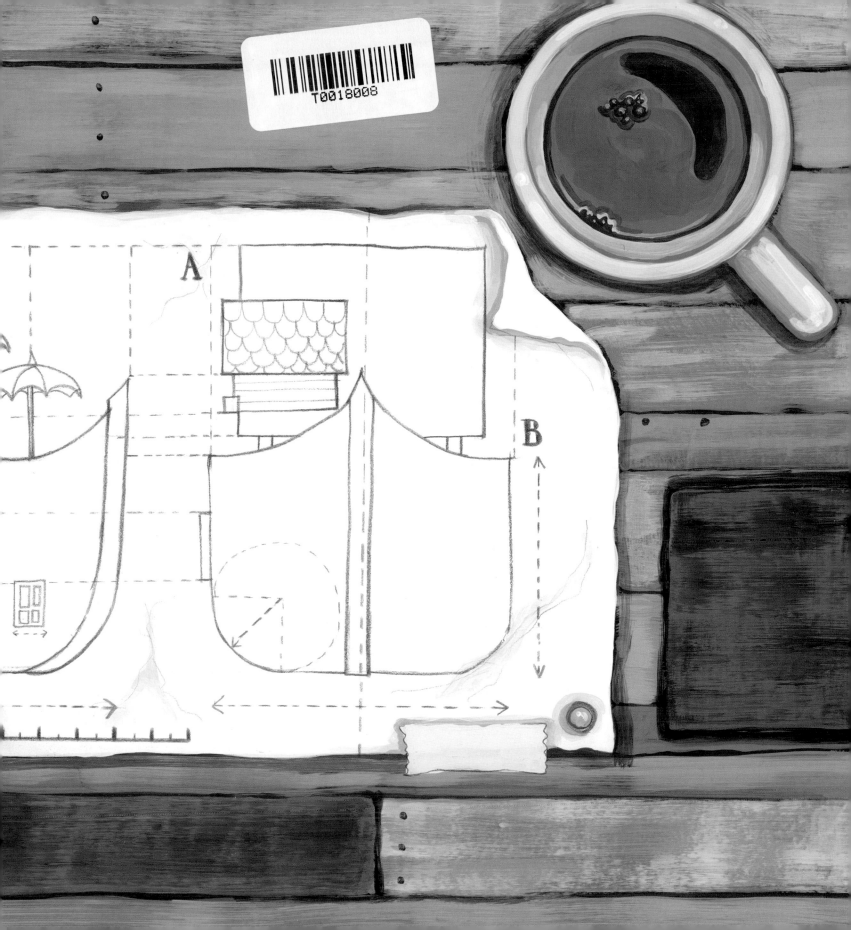

For "The Gang" – Amy, Steve, James, Em, Trude, Dave, Wend and Gerard. With love.

Text copyright © 2022 Ruth Hearson
Illustrations copyright © 2022 Ruth Hearson

This edition copyright © 2022 Lion Hudson

The right of Ruth Hearson to be identified as the author and illustrator of this work has been asserted by her in accordance with the Copyright, Designs and Patents Act 1988.

Published by **Lion Children's Books**
www.lionhudson.com
Part of the SPCK Group
SPCK, 36 Causton Street, London, SW1P 4ST

ISBN 978-0-7459-7952-6

First edition 2022

A catalogue record for this book is available from the British Library

Produced on paper from sustainable sources.

Printed and bound in China, February 2022, LH54

The Ark that Noah Built

Written and illustrated by

Ruth Hearson

LION
CHILDREN'S

This is the ark
that Noah built.

These are the animals who,

two by two, waddled and wandered,

followed and flew,

...onto the ark that Noah built.

This is the roof that covered and kept
Noah and his family safe as they slept, alongside
the animals who, two by two, waddled and wandered,
followed and flew, onto the ark that Noah built.

This is the rain that dripped and dropped –
for forty days it never stopped – onto the roof
that covered and kept Noah and his family safe as
they slept, alongside the animals who, two by two,
waddled and wandered, followed and flew,
onto the ark that Noah built.

This is the flood!

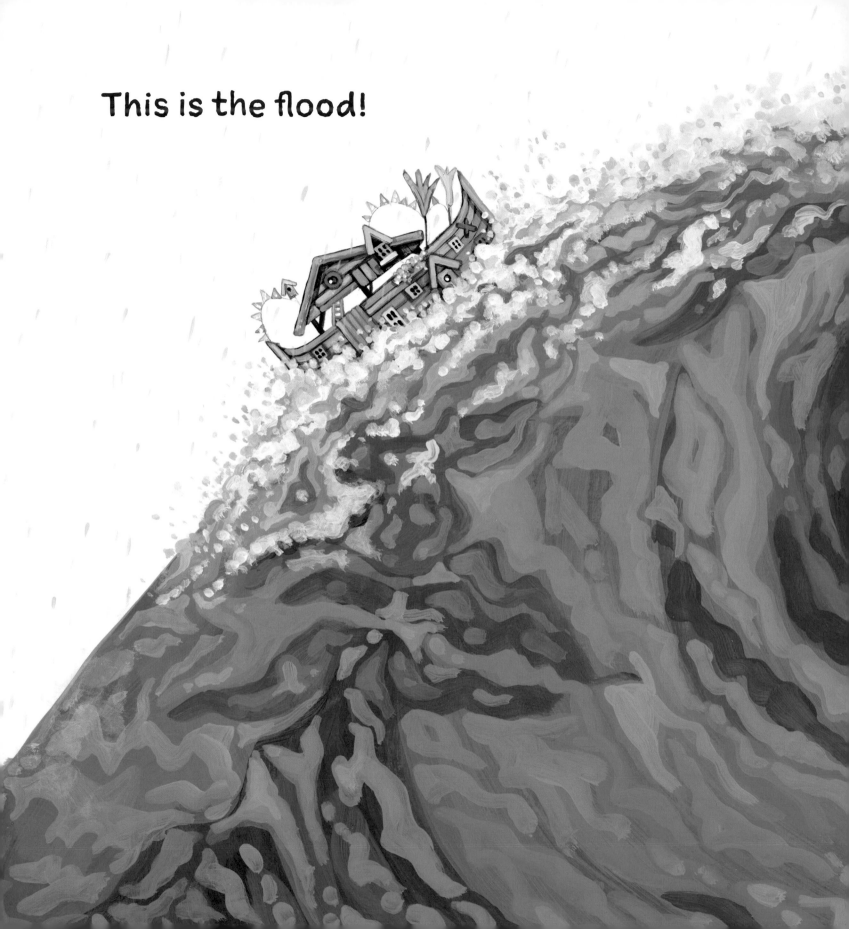

This is the flood that washed clean the land, making it new again just as God planned. He'd sent the rain that dripped and dropped – for forty days it never stopped – onto the roof that covered and kept

Noah and his family safe as they slept, alongside the animals who, two by two, waddled and wandered, followed and flew, onto the ark that Noah built.

This is the dove who, after the rain, went searching for dry land again and again. After the flood that washed clean the land, making it new again just as God planned.

He'd sent the rain

that dripped

and dropped –

for forty days it never stopped – onto the roof that covered and kept Noah and his family safe as they slept, alongside the animals who, two by two, waddled and wandered, followed and flew, onto the ark that Noah built.

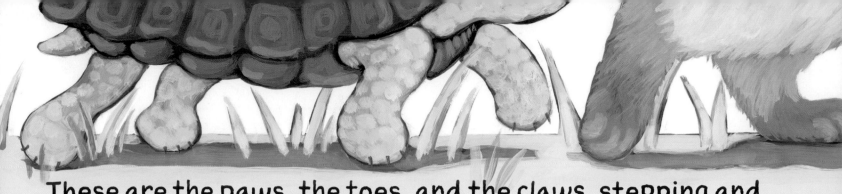

These are the paws, the toes, and the claws, stepping and skipping, no longer indoors. Thanks to the dove who,

after the rain, went searching for dry land again and again. After the flood that washed clean the land,

making it new again just as God planned. He'd sent the rain that dripped and dropped - for forty days

it never stopped – onto the roof that covered and kept Noah and his family safe as they slept, alongside the animals who,

two by two, waddled and wandered, followed and flew,

onto the ark that Noah built.

This is the rainbow!

This is the rainbow God put in the sky, a promise of friendship forever up high. To all of the paws, the toes and the claws, stepping and skipping, no longer indoors. Thanks to the dove who, after the rain, went searching for dry land again and again.

After the flood that washed clean the land, making it new again just as God planned. He'd sent the rain that dripped and dropped – for forty days it never stopped – onto the roof that covered and kept Noah and his family safe as they slept, alongside the animals who, two by two, waddled and wandered, followed and flew ...

...onto the ark that Noah built.